C000142100

A BOOT UP

CONSTABLE COUNTRY

Alan Casey

First published in Great Britain in 2014
Copyright text and photographs © 2014 Alan Casey

All rights reserved. No part of this publication may be reproduced,
stored in a retrieval system, or transmitted in any form or by any means
without the prior permission of the copyright holder.

British Library Cataloguing-in-Publication Data
A CIP record for this title is available from the British Library

ISBN 978 0 85710 083 2

PiXZ Books
Halsgrove House, Ryelands Business Park,
Bagley Road, Wellington, Somerset TA21 9PZ
Tel: 01823 653777
Fax: 01823 216796
email: sales@halsgrove.com

An imprint of Halstar Ltd, part of the Halsgrove group of companies
Information on all Halsgrove titles is available at: www.halsgrove.com

Printed and bound in China by Toppan Leefung Printing Ltd

Contents

Constable Country

How to use this book

The Area

The River Stour, gently meanders its way through the rolling Suffolk countryside. This wonderful river flows east from Sipsey Bridge 4 miles from its source in Cambridgeshire, along 8 miles in Suffolk and forms the county boundary between Suffolk and Essex all the way to Cattawade, its length totalling 68 miles long.

In 1795 this 'mighty river' was used as a canal and had 15 locks and the towpath crossed the river from side to side 33 times. Barges were drawn up the river by two horses which had to jump on and off the barges to be ferried across the river each time the towpath changed banks. Alas there is no longer a footpath which runs along all of its length.

The walks in this book starts from Bures and we cross from Suffolk to Essex walking in the footsteps of John Constable, our famous landscape painter, who gives his name to this, Area of Outstanding Natural Beauty, affectionately known as 'Constable Country'.

Routes and Maps

I have planned and walked all of the walks in this book, each walk follows public rights of way and permissive paths, all walks are circular bringing you back to your starting point. I have chosen each walk to start from either a small village or hamlet which is easy to reach by car.

Each walk is graded as either, easy, fair or more challenging. Facilities such as toilets, pubs, shops and post offices are mentioned, as well as distance in miles and km. Each walk is dog friendly but please have your dog on a lead when passing grazing animals and pick up your dog mess, there are bins for dog mess on most of the walks. Also mentioned is the type of terrain that the walks go over, as well as the grid reference for the starting point.

Whilst the maps give a basic view of each walk the text is written in a style which is easy to follow, however I recommend taking the relevant Ordnance Survey Explorer map (as mentioned in the text box) with you.

And finally each walk travels through the countryside that inspired Constable, from the rolling arable land and river valleys to the

magnificent and memorable Stour Estuary, I hope that you will be inspired.

Key to Symbols Used

Level of difficulty:

Easy 🍂

Fair 🍂 🍂

More challenging 🍂 🍂 🍂

Map symbols:

🚗 Park & start

⋯⋯ Walk route

━━ Road/track

━━ River/water

■ Building

✛ Church

🍺 Pub

Walk Locations

SUFFOLK

A134

A12

IPSWICH ●

① ② ③ ④ ⑤ ⑥ ⑦ ⑧ ⑨ ⑩

River Stour

Bures and Mount Bures Castle

A pleasant walk from Bures in Suffolk, over the River Stour into Essex and on to an ancient castle mound with magnificent views of the Stour valley.

Level: 🥾

Length: 3 miles (4.8km)

Ascent: 159.78 feet (48.70 metres)

Terrain: Country lanes, Arable fields

Park and start: Bures public free car park or side streets.

Grid Reference: TL906 340

Recommended Map: Ordnance Survey Explorer 196

Information: Pubs, shops, Post Office in Bures. WC only in pubs.

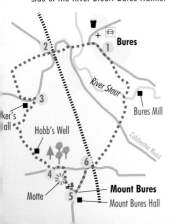

This walk is the first in this lovely area; it's an easy walk on the Essex side of the River Stour. Bures Hamlet our destination has the remains of a castle motte, known as Mount Bures Castle. A recent excavation in August 2011, led by Dr Carenza Lewis, well known from C4's Time Team, found that the medieval motte or mound was used as a lookout post.

① From the car park, turn left and walk back towards St Mary's Church, turn left at the road junction and cross the bridge into Essex. The bridge gives an excellent glimpse of the river here. Walk

St Mary's Church in Bures

towards the next road junction, on your right is the Old Toll House. Take the road on the right going straight down towards the railway bridge. Here is the local railway station. Pass under the bridge and on the right hand bend cross over to the lane on the left with a 'no entry' sign.

The Old Toll House

(2) This sign is for car drivers, so continue along this country lane with open fields on your right

Bures St Mary is a civil parish in the Babergh district of Suffolk. In 2001 the population was around 1800 people. The parish lies on both sides of the River Stour, Bures in Suffolk and Mount Bures in Essex.

and look out for the little wooden bridge which crosses a stream on your left, marked with a public footpath sign. Walk over this and walk uphill along the fenced-in field boundary. In the late summer the hedge on your left is full of blackberries. Go through the small gate at the end of the path and turn left on to a road, cross over to walk facing any traffic and on the bend take the farm lane on the right, signposted, 'Bakers Farm'.

(3) Watch out for the little Jack Russell here, who barks at you. Follow the farm lane ignoring the first footpath on your left, look to your left across the fields for a lovely view of Bures Mount Castle and Church. Take the next footpath on your left crossing over a field towards, 'Hobb's Well', and then passing a cottage on the right into a small wooded area, note that this woodland path could be muddy in wet weather. The short path reaches a small lane.

(4) Turn left here and walk along the lane crossing a stream, for a short distance going uphill, just before you reach the top of the hill take the kissing gate on your right which leads to Bures Mount Castle and Church. Walk across the field on

Mount Bures motte

Before the coming of the railway in 1849 heavy goods made in the village, such as bricks and malt, were transported by barge (lighter) down the river Stour to Mistley. The barges were pulled along by horses. John Constable depicted this in his paintings,'Flatford Mill' and 'The White Horse'.

the footpath towards the fenced in motte (mound). Walk around the fence and go through another kissing gate into the church grounds, this is the church of St John the Baptist.

5 After walking around the church go out of the main gate onto the parking area and turn

St John the Baptist Church

View from Mount Bures motte

In 1659 the village was also known as,'Bewers,' before it got its title of Bures.

left into the field, there should be details here about Bures Mount motte, walk along the field edge with the house on your left for a short distance until you reach the gate where you can walk up a flight of steps to the top of the motte, with magnificent views of the countryside below you. Then retrace your steps back to the church car park, turn left and left again on to a busy road. Cross over carefully to the right side and walk for a short distance facing the traffic into the village of Mount Bures. A village sign depicting a train and village history is on the left; cross

over towards it and walk towards the railway line.

6 Cross over the railway line and walking left cross the road to a track on the right, do not

Bures Hamlet, Essex

take the road on the right; the track is just past it. Follow this track with a lovely hedge for a short distance until it reaches the road again; turn right on the road for a short distance until you reach a T-junction. Cross the road to a footpath opposite, this pleasant track takes you down to a field gate. Veering left across the field towards the river Stour you are greeted with a magnificent view of Bures Mill, a scene straight out of a painting by John Constable. Unfortunately, the mill is in private hands and not open to the public. Walk across the

With the onset of the railway the slow river traffic went into decline and ended in the early 1900s.

footbridge, passing a weir on the left. Canoeist, have to get out of their canoes here and walk with them underneath the footbridge to reach the water in front of the mill. Continue

Bures Mill is one of the few remaining mills on the River Stour which once had 23 mills along its length.

An empty rowing boat on the River Stour, Suffolk.

on the way-marked track passing the mill; you are now on the Stour Valley Way, long distance footpath. Follow this way-marked route across a field back to Bures with the car park on your left.

Bures Mill

2 **Bures and Arger Fen**

For this second walk we start again from Bures with a walk along part of St Edmunds Way, a long distance footpath following rolling countryside to reach the Arger Fen, a small fragment of wildwood that once covered large areas of Suffolk over a thousand years ago.

B ures St Mary is the start of this second walk but the locals call it Bures. On this walk we explore the Suffolk side of the river Stour walking through the rolling countryside that John Constable knew.

Arger Fen

1 From the car park turn left onto the road and walk back into the village, on the right is the pub, follow the bend in the road and you will go past the Post Office and St Mary's Church. In a few steps you will reach the road junction; follow the road to the right

Level:

Length: 5.5 miles (8.8km)

Ascent: 221.13 feet (67.40 metres)

Terrain: Country lanes. Field paths and rolling countryside. Woodland.

Park and start: Bures public car park or side streets.

Grid reference: TL906 340

Recommended map: Ordnance Survey Explorer 196

Information: Pub, Shop, Post Office in Bures, WC only in pubs.

passing several old buildings. This is High Street. Follow the road around the bend passing the first road on the

Map labels: Reservoir, Farm, Farm, Farm, Chapel Barn Cottage, Farm, St Edmund's Way, Bures, B1508

Timber-framed house in Bures St Mary

right, then take the small lane on the right called St Edmund's lane.

 2 Walk along this undulating lane, passing several pretty cottages, for approx. half a mile until you reach a T-junction. Turn right here

St Edmund's Way, named after King Edmund, is an 88 mile long distance trail across Suffolk.

and follow this lane for a short distance until you reach the houses on the left. Just past the first house walk down the restricted byway on the left. This is a very pleasant walk along a country lane with views of the distant hills. Walk downhill on the

wide track passing Moat Farm on your left, and as the farm hedge ends at a field turn left and walk along the field boundary.

3 As you walk a short distance you will see a small reservoir

Cottages in Bures St Mary

A reservoir close to Bures St Mary

in the adjacent field on the left. You can walk into this field where you will find a convenient seat. You may see ducks and other birds on the water. Continue walking the bank of the reservoir and walk into the next field until you reach the little footbridge in the hedge on your right, walk over this and the follow the field with the hedge now on your left. As you reach

The rolling fields of Suffolk

the field end look into the left hand corner where you will find a metal kissing gate; go through this and with the hedge on your left walk over a wooden plank into the next field then after a short distance walk through the hedge on an 'official path diversion'.

4 Follow this path taking the right hand path passing another seat, walk again for a short distance until you reach a gate which leads you on to a tarmacked lane. Turn right here crossing over a ford on the little footbridge. The lane leads uphill here and you will soon reach

The ancient Arger Fen Woodland

the Arger Fen. This small woodland is just a fragment of wildwood remaining from the ancient wood which covered Suffolk; it is a site of Special

In Victorian times Bures was an industrial village, and self-sufficient. Its industries ranged from brick making, tanneries, maltings, and an abattoir and gas works. Several old buildings still remain.

Ford crossing near Arger Fen

A woodland creature in the Arger Fen Woodland

On Christmas Day AD855, Bishop Humbert of Elmham annointed a 14-year-old boy as King of the East Angles. The boy was Edmund, chosen heir of King Offa. His coronation is said to have taken place at 'Burva', known now as Bures.

Scientific Interest now owned by the Suffolk Wildlife Trust. You can walk around the woodland on various length walks; an information board tells visitors all about the woodland and its walks.

(5) As you come back out of the woodland continue walking left on the lane passing a lovely old barn in a bad state of repair. As you reach the bungalow on the right take the public footpath on the right down a leafy lane until you reach the field. Turn right and follow the field boundary for about 500 metres, looking out for the footpath sign on the right pointing into the field, this is the St Edmund's Way long distance footpath. Follow this across the field going downhill towards the hedge were you will find a stile in the hedge; cross this and walk uphill on a pleasant green track with tall trees on your left and superb views on your right of distant hills.

Old Barn near Arger Fen Ancient Woodland

Back in the 1950s Bures had several businesses including a bank, a Co-op, several shops and blacksmiths.

6 Walk through the farmyard towards the road junction, turn left here and then left again

on to a sandy lane, this is still St Edmund's Way footpath. As you go past the houses on your left take the track on the right, this is known as Sloane Avenue, were you will see a line of lime trees planted along the country lane. Follow this lovely lane downhill until you reach a small housing estate. Walk left towards the

main road; turn right here and walk for about 500 metres back to Bures car park.

In order to keep its workforce from dehydration the village once had more than eight public houses.

Sloane Avenue, Bures St Mary

3 **Wormingford**

From the village church where some of John Constable's relations are buried we follow country lanes and field paths around this delightful Essex hamlet – also the home of writer Ronald Blythe.

From the main gate, go to the right of the church where you will find the graves of John Constable's two uncles and their families. You will also find the graves of John Nash and his wife Christine; both were well known for their paintings of the countryside.

Inside the church you will find a colourful stained glass window depicting the story of the Wormingford Worm.

Level: 🥾 🥾
Length: 3.5 miles (5.7km)
Ascent: 176.84 feet (53.90 metres)
Terrain: Country lanes, field paths and rolling countryside.
Park and start: On roadside outside Wormingford church.
Grid reference: TL933 322
Recommended map: Ordnance Survey Explorer 196
Information: Local shop, pub and restaurant called the Crown, WC in pub

(1) Walk along the path on the left of the church; this is the Stour Valley Path. Go through the kissing gate, follow the track down and through the small woodland, reaching a field path which leads uphill along the field boundary, here

[map showing: Wormingford Farm, Wormingford Bridge, Farm, Weir, Cottages, Ash Grove Pond, Farm, Wormingford, with numbered waypoints 1–7]

Stour Valley landscape, near Wormingford

St Andrew's Church, Wormingford

Gravestone of William Death

The Grave of John Constable's Relatives

you will see magnificent views over the nearby hills of the Stour valley. At the top of this track you will walk through another kissing gate.

2 Turn right and walk along the field boundary until you reach another kissing gate in the corner of the field (do not go towards the kissing gate in the middle of the field boundary on your left). Go through the field corner kissing gate and walk towards the hedge in front of you. Walk to the left of this hedge and continue along the path for about 400 metres until you reach a stile on the right before the gate.

3 Go over this stile and follow the track uphill to the left of the field for about 200 metres where

The village name of Wormingford, recorded in 1254, gave rise to stories of dragons – worm meaning serpent or dragon. The stained glass window in the church shows a dragon being slain by Sir George Marney; George and the Dragon perhaps? It is however believed, in legend, that a crocodile escaped from Richard 1st of England's menagerie, making its way to Wormingford along the river Stour where it was killed.

will reach a gate, you may find the gate locked but go to the left and duck under the wire. This is church road, (right will take you back to the church) walk downhill to the left and follow the bend in the road to the left, in about 100 metres you will reach a bridge over the River Stour, lovely views of the river will be had here, also to the left is Wormingford watermill, now a private dwelling. From the bridge walk back uphill to the bend in the road.

(4) Turn left here along Bowdens Lane and then opposite the cottages follow the footpath sign across the field on your right towards the pylon and then the lone tree. Continue following this track into the next field, avoiding the footpath to your right. Caution should be taken here as there are numerous rabbit holes along this track. Continue across the next field towards the hedge where you will cross a wooden footbridge.

Poppy field Wormingford Essex

(5) Veering left across the next field, walk towards the distant farm buildings; you will reach another gap in the hedge with a footpath sign. You are now on the farm lane; follow this to the right up to and through the farmyard. At the crossroads turn right and follow the farm lane with oak trees lining its banks. The lane continues around a bend; avoid the footpath from the left, apparently this is closed on Christmas Day. Follow the lane uphill where in autumn the hedges are full of blackberries.

A Confusion of footpath directions

John Nash and his wife Christine came to live at Wormingford Mill in 1929 and painted numerous scenes of the countryside until John died in September 1977, aged 84, just a few months after Christine; they are buried in the churchyard.

An archaeological dig at Lodge Hills has found a lost Tudor hunting lodge where Queen Elizabeth 1st came to hunt in the deer park; a very interesting booklet about the dig is available to purchase inside the church.

(6) Just before you reach the left hand bend in the lane look out for the footpath sign on your right and another kissing gate. You will also see an information board about the Stour Valley Path which you have re-joined. Go through the kissing gate and walk to the right of the field for a short distance and then walk downhill across the field towards the kissing gate in the hedge. To your right is

A large number of finds from prehistoric periods suggests that the flood plains alongside the Stour held settlements long before the woodland was cleared on the hills.

Ashgrove pond with private fishing. Next to the kissing gate is an unusual water trough. As you go through the kissing gate go straight across the

A dog-friendly stile, near Wormingford

An unusual water-trough

field, veering left slightly towards the hedge with a stile which has a dog-friendly stile built into it.

 7 Follow the field edge up to the left towards the cottages and go through another gate, and straight up the track in front of you, passing the cottages on your right. Follow this fine wide track back towards church road and turn left to the church.

4 Nayland-with-Wissington

On this attractive walk we start from Nayland, where inside the church you can see a painting by John Constable.

Also on this walk we follow field paths and country lanes, cross the river Stour and visit the hamlet of Wissington with a return leg following the edge of the river bank back to Nayland.

(1) Park in Bear street in Nayland. From Bear street walk into the village which has numerous old buildings which are well worth looking at. Follow the bend in

The Old Merchant's House, Nayland

Level:
Length: 4.5 miles (7.2km)
Ascent: 131 feet (40.20 metres)
Terrain: Field paths, Country lanes, Village
Park and start: On roadside in Nayland
Grid Reference: TL974 343
Recommended map: Ordnance Survey Explorer 196
Info: Shops, Pubs, in Nayland. WC in pubs

the road to the right where you will see the church of St James. Inside the church you will see a famous painting by John Constable, 'Christ Blessing the Bread and Wine'. From the church

Timber-framed house in Nayland, Suffolk

through the hole in the hedge which leads to a seating area and another small footbridge. Walk over this; you are now in Essex. Walk straight across the left field in front of you to reach a gate. Cross the busy main road carefully to the footpath in the field ahead, this is the Anchor Inn Heritage farm footpath. Follow the footpath around the field edge until you cross over a farm lane then go through another hedge and cross over a quiet lane.

continue along the road towards Nayland Bridge, on the left next to the bridge is the Anchor Inn. Cross over the bridge where the river Stour flows beneath.

 When you have crossed the bridge take the little path

The River Stour and a dog walker

3 Once over the lane you are in a water meadow with several footpaths criss-crossing each other. We want to follow the signed Permissive Path veering left into an adjacent meadow which leads to a footbridge which crosses the river Stour. Then follow the track straight ahead with a lovely view of the privately owned, Wiston Mill. At the end of the track turn left. You are now on the Stour Valley Path; follow this path with enjoyable views of the River Stour on your left.

Wiston Mill, Wissington, Suffolk

The Constable painting, which hangs inside St James Church, 'Christ Blessing the Bread and Wine' of the Last Supper, is a famous portrait of Christ. It was commissioned in 1809 by John Constable's aunt who was living in Nayland at the time. The painting was stolen in 1985 but was swiftly recovered.

4 You will reach another small bridge on the left; this will take you to Little Horkesley if you wish, about a mile away. This is a small hamlet consisting of several houses, a church and the Beehive

View towards Wissington in Suffolk

public house. But we will continue past the bridge and follow the track towards the hamlet of Wissington, which is known locally as Wiston.

 At Wiston you will come to another church, this one

The village of Nayland and the hamlet of Wissington were originally two separate parishes. But in 1883 they were united into one civil parish, Nayland-with-Wissington.

dedicated to St Mary the Virgin. Inside this very old church is a wall painting of a dragon. Also in this church, as with many others, you will be able to purchase postcards, leaflets and the occasional booklet about the villages and the church, with all sorts of fascinating local information.

St Mary's Church, Wissington

The Wissington Dragon painting

6 From the church retrace your footsteps back to the Wiston mill junction, but walk straight on along the Stour Valley Path passing through several fields for about a mile; the river is across to your right. When you reach the road junction turn right.

7 This road leads to the main Nayland bypass. Carefully cross the road towards the village, then cross the next road to your right and walk towards the seating area on the green where you will see swans on the River Stour. Walk to the right with the river on your left and next you will see a bridge crossed over by the bypass. There is a footpath right beside the road going over this bridge; follow this and turn immediately left on to the path on the other side of the river.

St Mary's Church at Wissington (Wiston) is a true Norman Church, made even more Norman by an enthusiastic Victorian Vicar!

(8) Follow this path back towards Nayland Bridge and the Anchor Inn. If you are lucky you might see a passing canoeist. You will pass the backs of several houses with their very colourful gardens in summer, and the path overlooks a weir before you reach Nayland Bridge. The river however is still narrow in places. At Nayland Bridge turn left and walk back into the village to your car.

Canoeists on the river Stour at Nayland

The River Stour, Nayland

The Stour Valley path is a 60 mile route which follows the valley of the River Stour from Newmarket to the estuary at Cattawade. The walk passes through the landscapes which inspired the artists John Constable, Gainsborough, Munnings and John Nash.

5 Stoke by Nayland and Polstead

From the small hamlet of Polstead, we go on the trail of a grisly Victorian crime: The Murder in The Red Barn. Here, back in 1827, Maria Marten met her death. We walk along field edges, paths, country lanes and meadows passing the site of the Red Barn.

Level: 🥾 🥾
Length: 4.68 miles (7.54km)
Ascent: 186.02 feet (56.70 metres)
Terrain: Village, Field and meadow, lanes
Park and start: Polstead, outside Public House
Grid reference: TL993 383
Recommended map: Ordnance Survey Explorer 196
Information: Pub, shop and Post Office in Polstead. Pubs in Stoke by Nayland

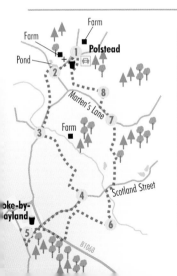

John Constable was a frequent visitor to the pretty village of Stoke by Nayland, he produced many sketches and paintings of the area, and our walk around the village passes many of these sites.

1 From the Cock Inn public house in Polstead walk downhill towards the village pond, passing Street Farm on your left, the large farmhouse is where William Corder lived. Corder was the son of a tenant farmer, and Maria Marten was the pretty daughter of the village mole catcher. William Corder and Maria were lovers.

Polstead Pond

A colourful Autumn scene

> *Polstead is famous for its cherries and gives its name to a variety, 'The Polstead Black'.*

yard of this 12th century Norman Church. But her grave has long since been plundered. From the left side of the church passing the war memorial, walk through the gate and down across the meadow heading for the gate on the right of the cottage ahead.

2 As you reach the pond turn right at the road junction and follow the pond fence around to its end where you go across the road and follow the lane up towards St Mary's Church. Maria is buried in the church-

3 At another road junction turn right for a short distance and cross the road to your left and go over a stile into another meadow, sign-posted Scotland Street. Follow the track keeping to the right side of the field. Just before you reach the field gate turn right at the footpath sign and follow the track uphill for a short distance and then turn left at the next field and follow its boundary towards the wood.

(4) Turn right on to the track leading through the small woodland to a lane, turn right and follow this lane to reach Stoke by

A leafy lane near Polstead

The Red Barn Murder was a notorious crime committed in Polstead in 1827, where Maria Marten was shot dead by William Corder, her lover. Her body was hidden in the Red Barn and Corder fled the scene of his crime. Maria's body was later found after her stepmother spoke of having a dream about her murder. Corder was later found in London and brought back to Suffolk, where he was found guilty of her murder and hanged in Bury St Edmunds. There is a leaflet available in Polstead Community Shop with further details about the murder.

A lady and her dog in Stoke by Nayland

Nayland. If you now walk across the road towards the Angel Inn and take the road to the left, follow this towards St Mary's Church passing several 15th and 16th century dwellings.

Stoke By Nayland village and church

The church of St Mary's,
Stoke by Nayland

Stained glass in St Mary's

The Church of St Mary stands on the highest point around and it appears in several sketches and paintings by John Constable.

(5) As you walk from the church grounds to the rear you will pass the town well, with the magnificent timber-framed Guildhall in front of you. Walk around the church and village; you will not be disappointed. There are several leaflets inside the church which refer to the history of the village. Retrace your steps back to the Angel Inn where you turn right into Park Street (this is the B1068 road), passing another pub called The Crown. Continue along a roadside path for a short distance until you reach the gate on your left. This is the Stour Valley Path. Follow this along

the field-edge, avoiding the footpath on the left, and continue along the field-edge over a stile and across another field to reach the fence.

(6) Turn left here along a fenced footpath towards the cottage, where you cross on to their driveway and meet a road. Turn right to cross the small bridge over the River Box, then turn left into a meadow passing through a kissing gate. Follow the path towards another kissing gate and a footbridge. Turn left and take the right fork at a path junction, climbing

The River Box

towards a small woodland. Once through the woodland you will meet a farm track with lots of wooden

John Constable was a frequent visitor to Stoke by Nayland and completed many sketches and paintings of the area. He wrote in 1830 about St Mary's Church: "the tower is its grandest feature, which from its commanding height seems to impress on the surrounding country its own sacred dignity of character."

fencing; follow the track keeping straight on as a path comes from the left towards Marten's Lane.

(7) Turn left on this lane, passing Cherry Tree Farm on your left; the lane goes downhill here. After a short walk downhill you will pass, on your right, Maria Marten's cottage where Maria once lived, and a little further on, Brook Cottage, where she

A Saxon Monastery was founded in Stoke By Nayland during the time of King Edmund.

was born. Return uphill and just past the entrance to Cherry Tree Farm take the footpath on your left and follow this into the field. Here stood the Red Barn where Maria's body was hidden.

Brook Cottage

The barn is no longer here, as it burned down in 1842.

(8) Continue along the path, going through another kissing gate. Follow the now enclosed track passing a small pond on the right towards another kissing gate into a field, veering right along the field path just past the stables on your left. The path goes through another kissing gate; follow this path back on to the Polstead Village Green and your car.

Maria Marten's Cottage

6 Stratford St Mary and Higham

On this short walk from the tiny hamlet of Higham we walk along riverside paths and meadows close to the River Brett to reach Stratford St Mary and return along parts of the River Stour via the Stour Valley Path.

The long street in Stratford St Mary is a reminder of its former coaching days when it catered for the many drovers of cattle, turkeys and geese bound for the London market.

(1) Our walk starts at Higham; parking is limited, so park next to the village green with its seat

Higham Village Green

Level:

Length: 3.75 miles (6.03km) or 5.08 miles (8.18km) if visiting Stratford St Mary's Church

Ascent: 76.77 feet (23.40 metres)

Terrain: Level walking across meadows and arable farmland and village lanes.

Park and start: Next to village green in Higham

Grid reference: TM034 356

Recommended map: Ordnance Survey Explorer 196

Information: Store, Post office and pubs in Stratford St Mary

around the central tree. From the green, walk downhill for a short distance back towards Thorington Street

John Constable completed a number of paintings in Stratford St Mary and the surrounding area, including a house in Water Lane. The old Stratford Mill, Dedham Vale, and the church are also featured in his works.

The landscape close to Higham in Suffolk

The Old Cottage, Higham

Higham Village is a Designated Conservation Area, located within the Dedham Vale Area of Outstanding Natural Beauty. It contains Rowley Grove, a nature reserve classed as Ancient Woodland.

village on the B1068, and just before you reach the bridge over the River Brett take the footpath on the left next to a delightful cottage, aptly named, The Old Cottage.

2 In a few steps the path leads you on to a meadow where you might see horses grazing. Follow the footpath across the next meadow towards the church on the right of the path. The river to your right is the River Brett, which at this point is about 400 metres north of the point where it joins the River Stour. The path crosses a lane and then goes via

The River Brett

a stile on to another meadow with metal railing.

3 Follow the path with the railing on your right towards another stile leading onto a track and then through a hole in the hedge. Keeping to the field on the left, follow the footpath with the wider track and

Stratford St Mary, in the heart of 'Constable Country' has a 15th century flint-faced church. It has traces of a henge from c. 4000BC, and Roman remains on Gun Hill.

hedge on your right until you reach a gate which leads on to a road.

4 Turn right on this narrow road and follow it around a left hand bend towards Stratford St Mary. Ignore the footpath on your left; this leads across an overgrown pathway with nettles. We however will continue on the metalled road until you reach an adjoining road, (not the road into a housing estate). At the road junction you can, if you wish, turn left and see the long street with several old houses and pubs and further still (approx. 1 mile) you can visit the Stratford St Mary Church.

5 Our walk will continue from this junction going right. Note the village sign on the opposite side of the road and the cold-looking concrete building on your right. After about 500 metres you will go past the Anchor Inn

Stratford St Mary

The Anchor Inn Pirate

on your left. Cross over to the right side of the road when you see the

In the Saxon period, the settlement had 30 tenants and a mill.

footpath which goes over a wooden footbridge over the River Stour, look to your left, this large area of water was used as a barge parking area.

 From the footbridge walk across the field veering right

The Black Horse public house has connections with the highwayman Mathew Keys, who was hanged on Kennington Common in 1751

Barge parking area at Stratford St Mary

Two swans on the River Stour

towards the field corner. This well-worn track is the Stour Valley Path. Go over the stile on to a path with views of the River Stour in both directions. After having only glimpsed the river on previous walks in this book, it's nice to follow the river bank here, but only for about 300 metres as our footpath turns off to the right at a footpath sign in the hedge. If you miss it you will run out of pathway. Follow the footpath now with a hedge on your right, passing to your right a large pond, usually with waterfowl. Continue on this path across two arable fields towards a gateway next to Low Lift Cottages.

(7) Turn right to cross over the River Stour on a bridge. After a short distance take the right fork at the footpath junction and follow this path across a couple of water meadows with several streams cut into the meadow; here you might see grazing animals. Go over the stile in the left corner of the field and follow the footpath around the field boundary going right and then at an adjoining hedge turn left towards the road. Turn right on the road, cross over the bridge and uphill back to the village green.

Water meadow near Higham

7 Dedham and the River Stour

This is the first walk where we now begin to see the River Stour in all its glory. We follow the footpath on each side of the river where pollarded willows line the bank, mirrored on the clear water, in the heart of Constable Country.

Our walk starts from the delightful village of Dedham, in Essex, which is set in the most beautiful

John Constable attended the village Grammar school in Dedham. He would walk to school each morning alongside the River Stour from his family home at East Bergholt.

lowland landscape. This area was a particular favourite of John Constable. Our walk and the next two will pass many places that feature in Constable's paintings.

Level:
Length: 3.5 miles (5.63km)
Ascent: 32.48 feet (9.90m metres)
Terrain: Riverside paths, meadows, village lanes
Park and start: In Dedham car park close to the River Stour
Grid reference: TM058 333
Recommended Map: Ordnance Survey Explorer 196
Information: Pubs, Café, Shops WC in Dedham. Boat Hire at Dedham

(1) From the car park next to the River Stour at Dedham Bridge, walk left into the village,

St Mary The Virgin, Dedham

Inside St Mary The Virgin, Dedham

Dedham Mill nearby was once owned by John Constable's father and features in Constable's paintings. Turn right at the High Street junction with many shops to explore. Opposite is St Mary's Church dating from the 15th century and inside is a painting 'The Ascension', by Constable.

Constable's 'The Ascension' in Dedham Churc[h]

St Mary's Church has a massive steeple which is a focal point of the surrounding Dedham Vale.

 After walking around the church and village make your way down the High Street (left from the road junction), passing several more old buildings until you reach the bend in the road.

3 At this bend, take the footpath straight ahead through a gate and follow it veering left across

Sir Alfred Munnings is another artist, with his famous paintings of horses, who had a strong connection with the area. Castle House, his home in Dedham, contains many of his works. His studio is also preserved here, and is open to the public. Munnings became President of the Royal Academy.

the field on to a driveway and then right to a small tree-lined track leading to the River Stour.

4 Upon reaching the river, turn right and follow the riverside path along for about a mile to reach a bridge. You will pass the site of a Constable painting, 'The Leaping

The Marlborough Head, Dedham

Dedham and the River Stour

Pleasure boat on The River Stour

In 1937 two artists, Cedric Morris and Arthur Lett-Haines founded the East Anglian School of Painting and Drawing at Dedham. Unfortunately the school burnt down and the studios were moved to Hadleigh in Suffolk.

Horse'. This lovely riverside walk passes several pollarded willows. You may also see several river craft and you will not be alone, for this is a very popular area.

(5) Walk over the bridge into Suffolk. You are now on the Stour Valley Path and St Edmund's Way, both long distance footpaths. Once over the bridge

When barges were pulled along the river there wasn't a continuous towpath along each side, so the horses were trained to jump on to the barge, which then ferried them to the other side of the river for their journey to continue. John Constable's painting 'The Leaping Horse', depicts this scene.

Rowing boat on the River Stour

Fen Bridge reflected in the River Stour

turn immediately left and follow the path along this side of the river all the way until you reach a gate onto the road.

6 Turn left at the road junction and cross over the Dedham Bridge. Note the lovely view up river from here. You can hire a rowing boat and stop for refreshments here. Follow the road back to the car park.

A line up of rowing boats at Dedham

8 **East Bergholt and Flatford**

From East Bergholt, John Constable's childhood home, we walk along field side tracks with views across undulating countryside down and along the River Stour to Flatford Mill, passing Willy Lotts cottage and several areas featured in Constable's paintings before heading back to East Bergholt.

This walk takes you on a journey through the pastoral landscapes of the Dedham Vale. John Constable (1776-1837) was born in East Bergholt. He became one of the greatest English landscape painters of all time.

Level:

Length: 3.76 miles (6.06km)

Ascent: 128.94 feet (39.30 metres)

Terrain: Field and riverside tracks, Village lanes

Park and start: East Bergholt car park

Grid reference: TM069 346

Recommended Map: Ordnance Survey Explorer 196

Information: WC. pubs, shop, tea rooms, restaurant in East Bergholt. National Trust Visitor centre at Flatford.

① From the car park turn right to walk past the Red Lion Pub, note the old house opposite with a sign, 'Maker of Hattes', on the wall. Take the lane on your right just past the village shop and Post Office. Here is John Constable's former studio, a quaint little building on your left. Continue along the lane passing a chapel and cemetery on your right and

The sign on Constable's Early Studio

49

John Constable's early studio

go through the gate to walk down the little track to cross over a footbridge at the bottom. A steady climb up the

path ahead gives you fantastic views over the Dedham Vale. The Steeple of St Mary's church in Dedham is across to the left whilst St Mary's in Stratford can be seen ahead.

2 At the end of the field track turn left and follow a leafy lane downhill, known as Dead Lane. Turn left again and follow the fenced-in track at the bottom of a field, passing

through a small woodland, veer right to cross a stile into another field which may have animals grazing, and follow the path across the field to another stile, before reaching Fen lane.

3 Turn right at the lane junction and cross over an old cart bridge with a lovely pond on your right. Follow the track for a short distance to reach the wooden Fen

Panorama of Dedham Vale

Along the river you will walk past many of the sites that John Constable immortalised in his paintings, among them 'The Cornfield', 'The Hay Wain', 'The White Horse' and 'Boat Building'.

Bridge, (which you crossed on the last walk). Walk over the bridge; here you will be greeted with magnificent views each way up and down the River Stour. Linger a while and take it in.

4 Once over the bridge, turn left and follow the riverside path as it winds its way to Flatford across the wide open pasture-land. Cross back over the river at the next bridge; you can hire a boat here if you wish.

At the road junction turn right and you will pass the National Trust shop at Flatford Mill. A little further on and the mill pond is reached, here is the famous, Willy Lott's Cottage, as depicted in 'The Hay Wain'.

Mill Pond and Willy Lott's Cottage

5 Follow the lane up past Willy Lott's Cottage, through the gate straight ahead into the field. Go straight on passing the track which joins from the right, then follow the left path uphill at the next path junction in the middle of the field. At the top of the field go through a kissing gate, and follow the fenced-in track along some meadows (often with horses grazing), until you reach a T-junction of footpaths.

6 Turn left here passing some farm buildings at Clapper Farm, to reach the farm entrance. Turn right at the road junction and walk uphill along the road. At the

In the churchyard is the medieval bell cage, erected here in 1531. The bells housed inside are some of the heaviest in England, weighing in at approximately 4.25 tons.

The East Bergholt bell cage

Site of Constable's childhood home

next road junction turn left passing the King's Head and the Haywain Restaurant. Continue along the pavement until you reach the churchyard of East Bergholt Church. Here you will find straight ahead the grave of Willy

Willy Lott's gravestone

Lott and to your right, in the corner of the churchyard, the graves of John Constable's parents Golding and Ann Constable. From the church stay on the right side of the pavement and walk back to the car park.

9 Cattawade and the River Stour

On this beautiful walk we start at Cattawade, where our lovely river continues its journey out into a long tidal estuary. But first we take a nostalgic walk back along its northern bank, to Flatford, and return along its southern bank through lush water meadows.

Level:
Length: 4.13 miles (6.65km)
Ascent: 19.69 feet (6.00 metres)
Terrain: Short lengths of road way, Water Meadow footpaths
Park and Start: Cattawade picnic site Grid Reference: TM100 331
Recommended Maps: Ordnance Survey Explorer 196,197
Information: Cattawade has a pub and Chinese Restaurant. Whilst at Flatford, the Bridge Cottage Restaurant serves lunches and teas.

The Stour was developed suitable for navigation back in the 18th century when barges carried goods all the way from Sudbury to Cattawade. But it fell into disuse by 1914. Now, thanks to the River Stour Trust, with its many volunteers the river has been given a new life.

① From the picnic site at Cattawade, walk back out to the B1070 (East Bergholt Road) and turn left to follow the pavement for a short distance passing some houses and a small industrial site. Then turn left onto an access driveway just past West Green Cottages, following the Stour Valley Path sign.

Bridge Cottage

Stour Valley Path

Cattawade

Flatford Mill

Manningtree Station

The Stour at Cattawade

2 After a short distance follow the path through a hole in the hedge on the right, beside a brick gate pier. Turn left on to a grassy headland with the hedge on your left. Soon you will go off to your left back through the hedge and then follow a path beside a wooden fence. At the corner of the meadow, go over a stile, where at this point you will see the River Stour. Walk straight on with the hedge now to your right. Continue across the next meadow and two close stiles with the hedge still on your right. Continue across several more fields and at the corner of the last field veer right to follow the Stour Valley Path sign towards a pylon.

3 Veering left, almost beneath the electricity pylon, walk

Awaiting a boat trip on the Stour

An 18th century bridge crosses the river creek at Cattawade and a John Speed, map of 1610 shows it as 'Catiwade Bridge'. Daniel Defoe even mentions it as being used at the time of the 1648 Siege of Colchester.

beside the hedge on the left, cross the stile in the corner of the meadow and veer left. After a few steps turn right on to a path between hedges, follow the Stour Valley Path signs to reach a wide track and walk left to go past Willy Lott's cottage and the Mill Pond. Follow the main track to reach Flatford Mill. Here you will find the National Trust Visitor Centre, Shop and Restaurant. You will also find an exhibition all about John Constable.

 Follow the track past the Mill and turn left towards the

A swan at Cattawade

Cattle on marshland near Cattawade

The 18th century, Old Cattawade Bridge

Mallards in a feeding frenzy

river, walk over the bridge and turn left to follow the river side path. This is part of the St Edmund's Way, long distance footpath. Flatford Lock is soon reached. Continue along the well-used path with the river on your left. You will soon reach a large con-crete structure of several sluice gates which serve to protect the meadows from flooding.

5 At the end of the structure we leave the St Edmund's Path to its journey to the right, whilst we go straight on to follow the path

In the nearby church at Brantham, another Constable painting can be seen: 'Christ Blessing Little Children'.

ahead on a raised bank, still with the river on the left. After about a mile we reach the busy A137 road.

6 Carefully cross the road and follow the pavement to walk over the 'White Bridge'. Continue along the pavement into Suffolk with views to your right of the Stour

Britain's first Xylonite (cellulose) works was opened in Cattawade in 1870 on a site off factory lane.

Estuary. After a short distance turn right at a road junction on your right and walk towards the Old Cattawade

Bridge, below you is another branch of the Stour were you will see water birds and the odd canoeist. Walk over the old bridge and follow the road through Cattawade Village passing the Crown Pub and The Chinese Restaurant and cross the main A137 again to reach the Cattawade picnic site.

Journey's end, canoeists at Cattawade

10 The Tattingstone Wonder and Stour Estuary

Birdwatchers will enjoy this walk as we head out to follow this majestic river along the shore of its tidal Estuary. Starting with a walk close to Alton Water, passing the Tattingstone Wonder we follow country lanes and cross farmland to reach the shore of the River Stour.

Level: 🥾 🥾
Length: 8 miles (12.88km)
Ascent: 108.92 feet (33.20 metres)
Terrain: Waterside paths, Country lanes, farmland tracks, and Estuary shore.
Park and start: Alton Water car park
Grid Reference: TM156 352
Recommended Map: Ordnance Survey Explorer 197
Information: Tea room and WC at Alton Water Car park.

Tattingstone was recorded in the Domesday Book as 'Tatituna' or 'Tatistuna'.

Alton Water was created in the 1970s to provide water for South East Suffolk. Water from the nearby River Gipping is diverted to fill it. It is a haven for water birds and sailing boats.

(1) From the car park walk to the left of the tea rooms out on to a pathway which is also used by cyclists. Follow the track to the left with magnificent views of Alton Water to your right. After a short distance,

Old tree skeleton on the Stour Estuary

The fine buildings of the Royal Hospital School for sons of officers and men of the Royal Navy and Royal Marines, was transferred to its present position at Holbrook from The Queen's House at Greenwich in 1933.

turn around and you will see the very tall Clock tower of the Royal Hospital School dominating the skyline. Alton Water supports many species of waterfowl and you will see large numbers of swans and ducks and if you are lucky you might spot great crested grebes, and cormorants. Follow the path and shoreline all the way up to and through Larch Wood after which you reach a fence.

Swan family on Alton Water

The Tattingstone Wonder

2 Go over the stile and turn left on to a country lane. In front of you is the Tattingstone Wonder. Built in 1761 this small group of workmen's cottages was built and disguised to look like a church by the local squire. Turn left along the lane and left again at the next road junction, follow this road up to the left hand bend.

3 Take the lane in front of you, passing Holly Farm. This little lane has holly trees along the

The Tattingstone Wonder and Stour Estuary

Boat at low tide

hedgerow which leads you onto the field edge path with lovely views of the field on your right. Turn right at the path junction and passing a solitary tree in the field you reach a small wood. Go on to the track and follow it to the left, passing several cottages up to the adjoining road.

(4) Turn right on to the road; this is Upper Street in the village of Stutton. Walk past the Gardeners Arms, where you could stop for refreshment, to reach the white gateposts of Stutton Hall. Walk down the hall's driveway. This is a pretty tree-lined avenue leading to the hall

in the distance with its tall chimneys. Unfortunately the footpath turns right about halfway down towards the hall, which is private.

(5) Follow the track passing a woodland on your left, turn left again on the next path junction

and around a bend towards Queech Farm; turn left onto the track just before Queech farm. As you follow this little track you will be greeted with distant views of the Stour Estuary. Shortly you will reach the gateway to Stutton Mill. Walk through the private grounds on a permissive path towards the bank of the Estuary. Walk up on to the bank and follow the track to the left.

(6) Across the Estuary you might see Thames barges moored at Mistley. Follow the bank along low cliffs and field edge paths with fantas- tic views of the estuary all along its edge. Passing woodland to your left you will be diverted on to the shore of the estuary. This is a delightful section with many waders seen feeding along the shoreline at low tide. When you reach Stutton Ness the shoreline path is diverted back to the main track

Stour Estuary towards Harwich

which passes the old wooden structure of Graham's Wharf below to your right in the water.

7 Follow the track left and then right. Look across the fields to your right and you will see the delightful, 'Crepping Hall'. Go straight on at the next path junction and go through a gate which leads onto the driveway to Crepping Hall, follow the path up and around the right hand bend and then left to follow a concrete driveway lined on the right with holly trees. At the road junction walk across the road and take the field edge footpath next to the cottage.

8 At the next junction of footpaths turn right and

Waders on the Stour Estuary

When Alton Water reservoir was created over twenty houses and two farms including Alton Hall disappeared beneath its waters. Alton Mill however was dismantled and re-erected at the Museum of East Anglian Life at Stowmarket.

follow this track passing some more cottages, and around the field edge until you meet another lane. Turn left and then right into another field. Follow this field path up to the main track and cycle path next to Alton Water. Turn right and walk back to the tea rooms for a well-earned cup of tea.